Know Your Numbers

From the Garden

A Counting Book About Growing Food

Thanks to our advisers for their expertise, research, and advice:

Stuart Farm, M.A., Mathematics Lecturer
University of North Dakota, Grand Forks, North Dakota

Susan Kesselring, M.A., Literacy Educator
Rosemount-Apple Valley-Eagan, (Minnesota) School District

by **Michael Dahl**
illustrated by **Todd Ouren**

PICTURE WINDOW BOOKS
a capstone imprint

The editor would like to thank Barbara Stendahl, Master Gardener coordinator for the University of Minnesota Extension Service–Dakota County, for her expert advice in preparing this book.

Managing Editor: Bob Temple
Creative Director: Terri Foley
Editor: Brenda Haugen
Editorial Adviser: Andrea Cascardi
Copy Editor: Sue Gregson
Designer: Nathan Gassman
Page production: Picture Window Books
The illustrations in this book were created digitally.

Picture Window Books
1710 Roe Crest Drive
North Mankato, MN 56003
www.capstonepub.com

Library of Congress Cataloging-in-Publication Data
Dahl, Michael.
From the garden : a counting book about growing food / written by Michael Dahl ; illustrated by Todd Ouren.
p. cm. — (Know your numbers)
Summary: Introduces the numbers from one to twelve as family members pick a variety of vegetables from the garden. Readers are invited to find hidden numbers on an illustrated activity page. Includes bibliographical references and index.
ISBN-13: 978-1-4048-0578-1 (hardcover)
ISBN-13: 978-1-4048-1116-4 (paperback)
ISBN-13: 978-1-5158-4092-3 (paperback)
1. Counting—Juvenile literature. 2. Vegetables—Juvenile literature. [1. Counting. 2. Vegetables. 3. Picture puzzles.] I. Ouren, Todd, ill. II. Title. III. Series: Dahl, Michael. Know your numbers.
QA113.D33 2004
513.2'11—dc22 2003020940

Printed and bound in China.
004708

Mama pulled ONE fat tomato
from the garden today.
one
1

Tony tugged TWO golden carrots from the garden today.

two
2

Sarah scooped up THREE red cabbages from the garden today.

Harry hauled FOUR heads of lettuce from the garden today.

four
4

Dad grabbed FIVE bunches of broccoli from the garden today.

five
5

Piper plucked SIX juicy strawberries from the garden today.

Grandpa picked SEVEN outstanding onions from the garden today.

seven
7

Grandma gathered EIGHT pods of peas from the garden today.

eight

8

Carl collected NINE cool cucumbers from the garden today.

9
nine
9

The twins rooted up TEN ripe radishes from the garden today.

ten
10

I carried ELEVEN perfect peppers from the garden today.

Now the family has TWELVE plates of spectacular salad

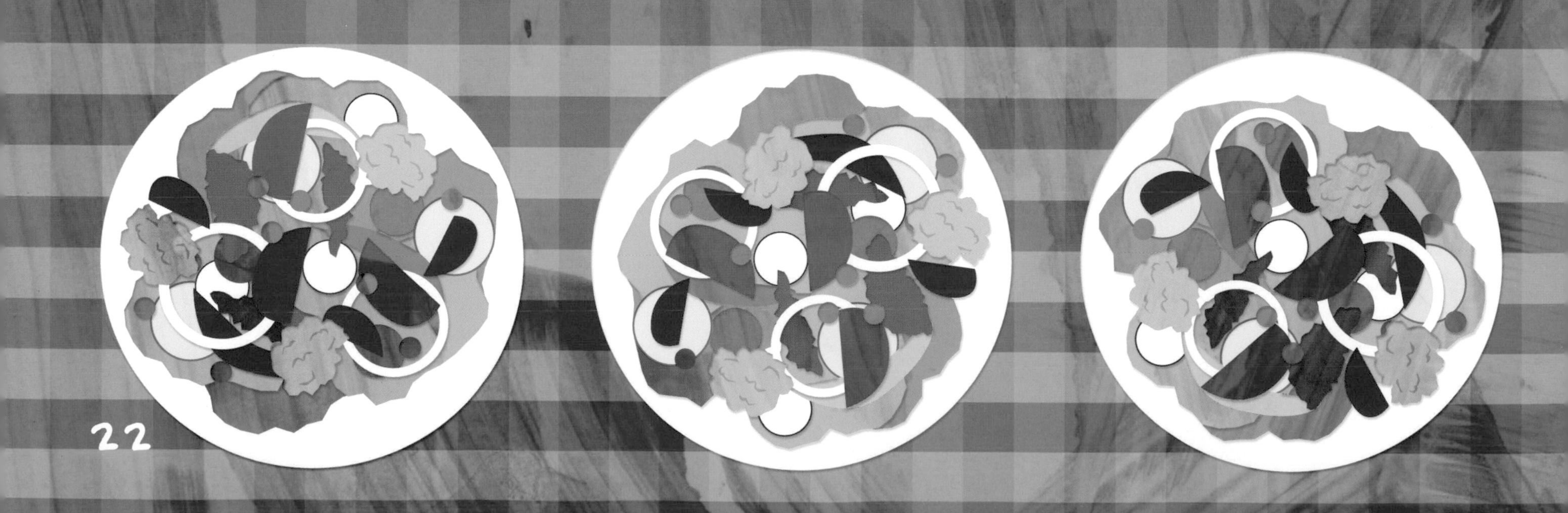

twelve

12

from the garden today.

Fun Facts

There are more than 4,000 different kinds of tomatoes.

The orange part of the carrot is the plant's root.

Red cabbage has leaves that are reddish-purple. The most popular cabbage is white cabbage, which has light green leaves.

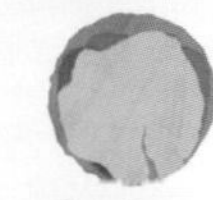

People have been growing lettuce for thousands of years. People in Persia may have been the first to have lettuce farms in 550 B.C.

Broccoli only takes about 110 days to grow from a seed into the broccoli you can eat.

Strawberries belong to the same plant family as roses do.

Look for all of the books in the Know Your Numbers series:

Ants At the Picnic: Counting by Tens

Bunches of Buttons: Counting by Tens

Downhill Fun:
A Counting Book About Winter

Eggs and Legs: Counting By Twos

Footprints in the Snow:
Counting By Twos

From the Garden:
A Counting Book About Growing Food

Hands Down: Counting By Fives

Lots of Ladybugs! Counting By Fives

On the Launch Pad:
A Counting Book About Rockets

One Big Building:
A Counting Book About Construction

One Checkered Flag:
A Counting Book About Racing

One Giant Splash:
A Counting Book About the Ocean

Pie for Piglets: Counting By Twos

Plenty of Petals: Counting by Tens

Speed, Speed, Centipede!
Counting by Tens

Starry Arms: Counting By Fives

Tail Feather Fun: Counting By Tens

Toasty Toes: Counting By Tens

Find the Numbers

Now you have finished reading the story, but a surprise still awaits you. Hidden in each picture is one of the numbers from 1 to 12. Can you find them all?

1 –stem of tomato
2 –in Tony's right ear
3 –holding girl's ponytail
4 –on the wagon's handle
5 –on the broccoli that is highest on the page
6 –on the basket's handle
7 –on shirt collar
8 –earring
9 –back of cap
10 –on radish row marker
11 –on farthest right yellow pepper
12 –in top left salad on page 21

On the Web

FactHound offers a safe, fun way to find Web sites related to topics in this book. All of the sites on FactHound have been researched by our staff.

1. Visit *www.facthound.com*
2. Type in this special code: 1404805788
3. Click on the FETCH IT button.

Your trusty FactHound will fetch the best sites for you!